nakamowin' sa for the seasons

nakamowin' sa for the seasons

RITA BOUVIER

thistledown press

Thistledown Press Ltd.
410 2nd Avenue North
Saskatoon, Saskatchewan, S7K 2C3
www.thistledownpress.com

Library and Archives Canada Cataloguing in Publication

Bouvier, Rita E., author
Nakamowin'sa for the seasons / Rita Bouvier.

Poems.
ISBN 978-1-77187-055-9 (pbk.)

I. Title.
PS8553.O8893N35 2015   C811'.54   C2015-900487-X

Cover drawing detail, *Fort de l'Île-a-la-Crosse*, 1820, by George Back
Cover beadwork, circa 1830s, Métis, artist unknown (collection of the Manitoba Museum)
Cover and book design by Jackie Forrie
Printed and bound in Canada

Thistledown Press gratefully acknowledges the financial assistance of the Canada Council for the Arts, the Saskatchewan Arts Board, and the Government of Canada through the Canada Book Fund for its publishing program.

I realized that man's artistic creations and his dreams, often resulting in beauty, as well as his fumbling toward God, must be primal, possibly the result of the biological urge which inspires the wood thrush to sing and the coyote to talk to the moon.

— John Joseph Mathews. (1945) *Talking to the Moon.* University of Oklahoma Press

CONTENTS

takwākan — Autumn

pipon — Winter

how do we hold silence

how do we hold silence
in lines of poetry, in the syntax
of the poem's phrases or sentences?

and, why does it matter anyway?
is there not more power
in the words we write,

in words we say to each other?
touched, our being, lifted, soars.
nisimis, I say in relationship, *cry.*

there is no shame in loss,
in a heart full of love —
our dad gone to the spirit world.

astam, let me hold you.
but not too tightly, you joke
but words can also hurt

leave us behind.
a freckle-faced young man on the bus
into Calgary, oozing the last call,

is initiating his travel companions
with Indian names for all to hear.
comes-too-quickly, I should laugh.

smashed-in-the-head, I cringe.
I wish I were somewhere else,
his travel companions trying to shush him.

sīkwan — Spring

taking a deep breath, I cover my face
with my shawl, beseech
sleep to come quickly

as antidote for the young man's transgression.
once spoken, words cannot be taken back.
sure, there is always the word *sorry*.

but listen to the sound
it makes, a pathetic overture
of could have — should have.

but silence   left as space
between our words can hold
everything and more; it holds its own.

it becomes the measure
of the sacred space between us —
the uncertainty of our knowing

and there are no words for that.

sīkwan — Spring

into the mouth of *misinipî*

stroke upon stroke in a song-like rhythm
the men dip their paddles into the churning waters;
the skimming bows of their canoes gliding
over the lake into the mouth of *misinipî*.

sâkitawahk is behind them, now; safe.
kisîmanitô has shown kindness once again
bidding the wind to rest, to let his people pass.
there, they pause, hats off   heads bowed.

silence   graced by the splash of water
      playful pelicans dipping for food.
kiýâsak in friendship dive to catch a few scraps.
fish swallowed whole into the mouth.

sīkwan — Spring

songs to sing

it was here in the Northwest,
the free traders and coureur de bois
of the XY, Northwest and Hudson's Bay companies
arrived from the east singing their songs,
searching for riches the land held.

it was here they stayed, were swallowed
into the place of no good-byes;
just *kitahtawî kawâpimtonaw* —
a humbling gesture to the energy of
this place that gives and takes on its own terms.

it was here they learned the importance of
wahkohtowin from our mothers — fire keepers,
who knew *askiya*'s contours and medicines
feeding the body, the mind and the spirit.
reverence, not too strong a word for its generosity.

here in the Northwest,
the free traders and coureur de bois
voyaged the York boat brigades each spring;
no river or portage ever too long
or arduous, as long as they had fifty songs to sing.

it is said that as they launched their boats
white pelicans soared above them in kinship
for their journeys up and down the *misinipî*, north
to the McKenzie, northeast to Hudson's Bay, sometimes
southeast to *kihcikamī* and west to the Rocky Mountains.

wingtip to wingtip they flew directly above paddlers
like veteran pilots on a mission, bidding farewell — a safe journey
down the waterways, the rapids like wild white horses and snakes.
and then, it is said, the pelicans soared back again
on reconnaissance   returning to their flock.

sīkwan — Spring

it is said that by day they were accompanied
by the mnemonic sonic songs of
kiŷâsak — gulls, *les cilowî* — sandpipers
terns and shorebirds of all kinds;
the men paddling in perfect time   fifty songs to sing.

it is said that by night, they were guided
by a new silver moon as it paled —
hallowed be thy name. all the while
the waves cresting over sparkling rough waters;
the paddlers mesmerized   fifty songs to sing.

it was also here in the Northwest,
the free traders and coureur de bois fought family
in competition for rich furs
until trade   and then food declined;
the land exhausted   no song to sing.

a new way of being arrived, a slight shift in the wind —
an ominous hush telling of what was yet to come.
when it came, they say
it blew in from the south — *sāwanohk ohci*
hungry, feeding like a wild man-animal —

piyakwan wihtikō wīnō.
it gorged itself, eating
oils and minerals, diamonds   and spirits
with which it is blessed *holy Mary,*
mother of God, wīcihinān — help us.

still though, when the wind rests for the night
and the moon comes out to show her shine
slip-sliding, shuffling across the night sky
to an old paddling song from days gone by,
you too, will hear the chorus line they sing,

alouette, gentille alouette,
the paddlers on their way home their flock awaiting.

sīkwan — Spring

at Granville and West Georgia

from her seat on the sidewalk café
she could see him coming a distance away,
in a coat of many colours and flowing ribbons.
he is feeding birds and gazing at the building and clouds.

he stops at the corner of Granville and West Georgia,
an overgrowth of dark steel and glass
obscuring the light of the day. birds flying by sonar.
sky-mirrored windows deceiving — deadly.

there, he shakes his head and ruffles his ribbons
before continuing on his way, walking stick in hand
guiding him through the traffic and the noise.
steel, concrete structures transforming in his path;

now, tall cedars — waving their arms in the ocean breeze
lifting, lifting their faces skyward to embrace
their power — *how the raven stole the sun.*
she imagines he is praying for rain   the rotting decay

as he dances to the rhythm beneath his feet.
across the sidewalk he swirls, full body in motion,
then stops to gesture — to bow in reverence
to the birds and squirrels foraging for food.

she watches passers-by avoiding him
as he talks to himself and to the heavens;
and, like zombies out of some B-movie
their eyes glazed straight ahead, they pretend

not to notice him   or each other,
as they clutch their morning coffee,
on their way to work.   she wonders why
we are so afraid to make eye contact.

she thinks: maybe we are afraid
to fall into that deep dark well — recognition.
our differences kaleidoscopic — of one light.

Indigenous man 2
(for Sherry Farrell-Racette)

she says   the love of the Métis
woman   is worn on the body
of her Métis man   adornment
like a wild Rose   on a lapel

but here   a flower is distinctly stitched
as protection   from the wilds
as invocation   for a safe journey
as a love   like no other

elemental   without bounds
in a blue of infinity

ten turned sixteen

1

you are the creation of two tiny cells
attracted like the magnetic pull of
two powerful forces — the north and south pole,
swimming your way into being — a fish.

a fish with arms and legs, and a head
so round, ready to make the journey home.
your mother and father waiting — counting
a second with each breath, a breath in — out.

time ruptured by a wailing call, you fell
into the outstretched hands of a waiting
nurse — a grandmother of ancient times.
you peed all over the nurse — a son, we heard.

in my arms, I counted your tiny toes;
I counted your fingers; your eyes.
eyes closed, your pursed lips awaiting, hungry
sucking to your heart's content!

2

we took you home, unsure what to make of
you, your constant cries of hunger, your constant
call for care, love and understanding. small,
you were so small. disarmed, we fell in love.

opening your eyes you cooed and cackled
echoing each breath and sound you could find,
human, bird, animal, insect, wind and thunder
until the day you discovered the sound *dada,*

and then *mama*.
soon, you were rummaging through the cupboards
the colourful toys, stuffed animals pushed aside
stacking pots and pans was making music.

you wanted to be where the action was —
the kitchen. the tiny bathroom a special place
water sounds splashing, swooshing, sloshing.
your presence and smile always a constant.

3

it was no accident, when you decided
it was time to take the very first step,
pushing aside the guiding hands keeping you
steady, fell, stood up and tried again.

and then you were everywhere. no fence
could keep you in or out — to mom and dad's,
Glady's dismay. the rolling balls your guide
and batter to beat a playground — a mimic.

quickly, you learned the power of saying
"no!" to every request made of you. bribery
too strong a word for give and take, take and
give. intelligent, you caught on, thank god!

next, you were chasing butterflies and bees,
catching the storm from the veranda
safe in your mother's arms, the sky alive
lightning and then thunder waiting for rain.

4

you dance in the rain, you swim in puddles
an inch deep, but no matter it was joyful
while it lasted. a towel always ready
to devour you when it was time to come in.

sīkwan — Spring

then came Dontello, Michelangelo
and all his turtle buddies from god knows where
chasing rats. down the sewer they would go.
you, as narrator, always wanted to follow.

thank goodness for imagination, *wihtiko*
moved to the city, to the dark alleys
from the bushes of northern Saskatchewan,
where it had been in hiding for some time,

waiting for just this moment. no fear
you were certain you could fly,
leap from the tallest buildings, land
in one piece regardless of the circumstance.

5

you are ten turned sixteen.
nothing we do can will stem the flow of time.
once upon a time you were captive in our arms
now we must let go. it isn't as easy as it looks.

tonight, I watch you get ready to step out
into the night. I hesitate to say a word
of caution. cocky at sixteen. I whisper
in relationship, *nigosis, papīyāhtak!*

transcending time

what a beautiful piece, the woman says
admiring my pendant.
          my eyes dancing
I tell the story of the double-headed, infinity serpent
I wear around my neck as protection,
a story of friendship cast on Turtle Island
which moves across the sea to Aotearoa–
land of the long white cloud
to the land down under,
the big island of Hawaii and then
to the northern plains of Russia,
to the mountain tops of Peru,
to tribal lands of Northern India.

I pause —   a way of speaking.
the woman filling the void, says:
it's too bad the only stories
out there   about Aboriginal people
are negative ones;   sad ones, really.

in this frog moon, I rise trembling,
continue my story   in friendship
          transcending time.
two carved out *waka taua*,
each carrying fifty men,
are advancing to the shoreline
paddling in unison,
as they sing a greeting song
for their guests from around the world —
Waikota River amplifying their song.

sīkwan — Spring

upon its shore they begin an ancestral dance
of *haka*, challenging our intentions to their land,
gestures threatening, weapons in hand.
     recognizing us as friendly,
they place a symbolic offering
on the earth.   disarming, they greet us:

breath on breath.

sīkwan — Spring

the mighty *Waikota*

the mighty *Waikota* winds its way snaking
down the mountains and through the valleys
and nothing, nothing can stop it from its course,
its course to the open sea.

all the moon can do is cling,
cling to the heavens returning a promise
of spring. birds of all wings and colors are gathering
twigs, discarded fluff and glue of nature's very own.

the mighty *Waikota* knows
no other course other than this one,
shifting and meandering here and there,
a certain order deep at its core.

the seeds transported to valley of the *Waikota*.
have fallen to a state of completeness
taking hold of the moisture, soil replenished —
nutrients for their small feet   they find ground.

sīkwan — Spring

stopping for eternity

she meanders the paved foot path
along English Bay in Stanley Park
sunset dreaming;

she comes upon a man, fifty something.
he is standing on the rugged shoreline
in depths of no return

rocking back and forth; roses in his arms
like he never wants to let go;
precious Fuchsia.

slowly, ever so slowly
he releases his hold   casting one
and then the other to the open sea,

when he comes to the last one
          he stops for eternity;
and then   finally lets go.

she wondered if it was true
that we see things as we are
and not really   as they are.

and, then unannounced —
a sudden release of pain —
so close, it just missed her heart.

sīkwan — Spring

a day past forgiveness

lately she finds herself walking
walking around in circles
tip toeing   trying to avoid minefields
          of worldly matters:
whose name will appear first on the line,
alliances — who's friends with whom?

she knows all are born of a knowing —
a binary world — they can't seem to escape;
here, on this page and in their bodies.

this morning, a day past forgiveness,
the first rain came pit, pit, pit, pattering
against her window pane; *î pôwâta.*

she could hear grandfather's hushed voice,
*nitânis . . . she's decided to clean house,
her helper, oŷôtin, won't be far behind.*

*I'm going to tie the boat and tent down;
stay warm, we won't be getting far today.
I will make a fire to keep us warm.*

they had been journeying down the river
to visit relatives — *opâsîwînowak* —
they had not seen all winter long.

as the sky darkened, the temperature dropped.
she slid deeper into the down-filled cover,
wrapped in an extra layer —

          a blanket of relationship.

don't cry for me
(for Verna)

tonight, eyes down, we pray for Virgil
as he lies at rest, an angel by name only.
his passing laying bare our own lives
sometimes more raw and fragile than
we would like   in a public space.

tonight, in vigil, comes a wailing
from the deep; heads bowed
there is no gaze to hold. only arms
to surround and comfort one another.
a ritual we partake in too often.

motionless, unconstrained, he is free.
free from his struggles, free from the sadness
the world heaps on dark, vulnerable spirits;
free from the addictions of life — a toll;
a toll he paid for all our sins.

in the depths of sorrow comes the tender
whispering, *don't cry*   *don't cry for me.*
just then, *the old ones* descended over the city
a ribbon dance of swirling twirling reds and yellows
dancing our sorrow — dancing our ache

into a wholeness   of being.

sīkwan — Spring

under the cover of rain

searching   I leave for an early morning walk
trying to follow the path — the narrow one
called *the red road,* a hard one to follow
on most days, but I try anyway   prayerful.

I head to the Harbour Centre   a good place
to start on this grey, rainy spring day.
I brace myself for the inevitable —
witness to the fallen angels in doorways

who are seeking warmth.   images too much to hold
too many sisters and brothers lost   to the streets.
the rain is coming down in sheets
and gulls are calling *kiýâs, kiýâs, kiýâs.*

as I walk the water's edge   I remember
skipping stones along the shoreline with my cousins;
singing   singing to the stones   skipping stones,
how many children will I have?

not knowing the significance of my song.
today   I am grateful.
the rain is pouring down as I take the hill at Bute,
a four gallon jug of water strapped to my back.

my brother John is carrying a willow whip
striking it in the air to keep me and my younger sister
on the count,   *you can do it*, he says,
you can do it!

I hold him close.   on Robson, I head north
to the crossing at Denman, a path I know
will take me to English Bay, to the anchored boats
who have journeyed here across the Pacific.

sīkwan — Spring

rain a trickle, I stand still in homage to place;
an invocation to the cedar spirit
inhaling her scent   her breath of life.
        I am thankful.

head down, I turn south and east along False Creek;
a watershed of an ancient rainforest
streaming to the open sea.

sīkwan — Spring

for sale

thanks for the warning,
the rain of love to ease the coming down
from heights of snow-capped mountains,
soaring solitary eagle flights.

maybe it wasn't a good decision
to have a glass of wine
with my tortilla soup after all;
but I wanted to extend the glow,

the orgy of poetry and mountain air.
recount the gems I collected along the way.
enjambment taking us to . . .
unknown territories.

the ghazel, *couplet like*
tips of trees rising
out of water. punctuation . . .
is punctuation. need I say more?

the servitude of emotion
for the poem and only the poem.
and, if the poem isn't working
begin with the last line.

words.   just remember
every   single   last   one
is important. turn each one
over and over again.

kill the darlings!
erase your footsteps!
get out of the poem!
listen deeply, be still —

dadirri, I whisper to myself,
when the call of a gate change
for passengers heading to Saskatoon
reminds me I am at the Calgary airport.

I rise slowly taking that last sip,
head to gate 50, my brown leather-bound
notebook clutched close to the heart.
the next moment though is unclear

when I suddenly find myself
sobbing at the site
of authentic Indigenous goods
for sale, recalling:

every word counts.
it's *The Trading Post* Rita,
get a fucking grip on yourself
people are watching you

fall apart, unravel
the mystery of your circumstance.
a pretty mukluked brown faced
doll dream catching,

amidst an abundance of
real stones, gems and turquoise.
moose jerky and token animals
is not the real thing.

the new-aged sounds of nature,
the ancient drum songs
on a hard pressed disc,
near a reel Indian

head-dressed next to the Inushuk
are made in China,
for God's sake.
take flight and just remember:

what is not for sale.

one morning after the rain

her breath a whisper she awakens her brood
wild creatures in first light, her offering
a song of songs   only birds can sing.
hillside, a light mist clings, covering her face.

the early light catches each strand   of grass
swaying in the breeze   imitating the flow of life.
the grass dance is sure to begin, but not
until the night hawk on his perch   rests.

in glory blood red, sky blue, grass yellow
dancers will whirl and whirl and whirl a circle
in honour of her beauty.   humbled.
a winged mid-flight embrace of birds is a reminder

they know this place better than anyone. she cries
in relief when rains come, knowing all is well.

little lemon yellow sailboat

eyes half open, I awaken
bright morning light streaming
through the window overlooking the Gorge.

on the far bank sits
a little lemon yellow sailboat
marooned   no owner in sight.

my heart skips   remembering
that little rowboat with oars
my papa built   sized to fit.

to a la Grosielle I would row,
embarking on many as trips as necessary
to carry all my cousins to the tiny island.

the island a perfect size for children
to wander — to play on the sandbars
with pelicans and gulls all day.

across the way, under a canopy of pines
the figure of a man rises.
in slow, measured time

he walks over to the lemon
yellow sailboat on the shoreline
its paler yellow sail in the wind.

there is a glint of something shiny —
a ceremonial movement
of hand to mouth as he drinks.

he stands still for the longest time
looking down the inlet and then
walks the perimeter of his sailboat.

nēpin — Summer

he climbs in, places the bottle on the ledge,
and begins wringing a rag over the edge.
done, he returns to the shaded canopy.

there, he sits waiting . . .
while I drift into the blue beyond   floating
in my little rowboat   borne up into clouds.

nēpin — Summer

thank god for waiters
(a poem never surrendered to Kateri Akiwenzie-Damm's
call for Indigenous erotica)

she is always in control, at least in public
today is no different. she sits   in a square
hoping to stem a certain tide to come.

she had not seen him for some time, and now
he sits there, last night's dreaming,
a deep throbbing ache.

it's true then, she tells herself, it's true;
that ache doesn't lie, nor can his eyes;
his eyes which say it all   he wants her.

sipping his wine, a Chardonnay from the valleys
of a faraway land, he motions hand in the air.
bravado!

the waiter stops to ask, *can I get you another glass, sir?*
          just that moment the aching subsides.
thank god! thank god for waiters!

and, then it starts all over again, as he rides every move;
every move she makes a trigger, a coded ancient language
without boundaries; space is time   without end.

he touches her ever so slightly each time she reaches out
to stroke the stem   of the glass of red wine, her fingers
lingering   she licks her lips before she takes a long sip,

               not wanting, ever
to finish that earthy, supple glass of wine.

~ 32 ~

nēpin — Summer

we must make something of this earth

the young ones are born
woven in the fabric of the present day.

they fashion their lives according to the latest
hip-hopped, low-bottomed swinging

designer jeans. the boys tilt their hats
to one-side to say   *I am hip.*

the girls adorn flimsy I-am-woman
garments that say   *it is springtime —*

the frenzy of nature in the air,
the young ones haven't yet figured it out:

why the robins are hastily building their nests
tucked safely in the crook of a branch,

why the little flowers along the roadside
bloom radiance — their fragrance in the air,

their nectar attracting bees and insects
and even the old lovers passing by.

they have yet to read Pablo Neruda
we must make something of this earth

because unto this planet we were born.
compelled, they will feel the need to leave

something behind, they can't escape it.
the code written into their blood.

there are cemeteries
(for Marilyn in Toronto)

and then   there   are   cemeteries.

they are the closest we have to green,
she says with her worldly flair,
hair brushed sexy to the side over one eye.

quiet really and one doesn't have to wait.
there is always an empty bench to sit on,
even here   poetry comes to you!

in Northern Saskatchewan, they are next to
the best story the land has to offer, I say.
an open book of truths and half lies.

in this small village, there are two, no three,
four plots of land to rest the weary
on their journey home.

at Mckay Point lie the unrepentant sinners
and protestants; sure as hell, most know where
they are headed.

at rest, sleeping in God's hand are: Wm Nichol;
Elias Dirikson Rimstad; Elnar Johan Pederson;
Thomas Robert Middleton; Hugo Soonum of Norway.

count me in I say, because sure as can be
there will be a perpetual party. dancing!
singing! I couldn't imagine better company.

at the cemetery proper of this small village
over in the far, far corner, once gated,
is the resting place of the little ones.

never had a chance to see the light of day.
they are forever in Limbo; never shall they
see Purgatory, Heaven or Hell. poor babies!

nēpin — Summer

on the knoll overlooking the cemetery are the believers,
a gated community of the blessed and holy
whose constant prayers have paid off:

our dear Seour Therese Arcand, Brother Guy,
Father Rossignal and our beloved Seour Riel —
sister to one rebel Canadian hero, Louis Riel.

in the rest of the cemetery, lies the pitiful
but repentant sinners; masterful storytellers, really!
with a little libation and a slippery tongue,

they could make up sins on the spot
in the confessional before Sunday mass. *tâpwî!*
in this tradition, it is important to underscore truths.

father, please forgive me for I have sinned.
I have erred telling a few white lies to my parents,
and hurling blasphemies in vain in the wind.

I have sinned most gravely against my neighbour.
that dirty asshole can't keep his dogs at bay.
mon Dieu! Jesus-Marrî-Joseph!

for sinners who are also believers, there is no certainty.
the gatekeeper in the end will decide;
this is surely the best story of all.

who will enter the pearly gates to heaven
or spend time in purgatory on their way
to heaven or simply go straight to hell?

here, every repentant sinner
wants to be buried with a gallon jug of wine,
            and rosary, just to be sure.

on the seventh day
(in memory of my Auntie Pauline)

we awaken, knowing
that going to mass is just the first step.
the priest's elongated singsong

in nominee Patris et Fillii et Spiritus Sancti
is a prelude for a family ritual
on this hot, August day.

red Shamrock lard pails in hand
vegetables pulled from the gardens
we pile into brightly coloured boats

with thoughts of northern pike
on a cross-stitched spike of some sweet sapling
barbequing over an open fire

but — not until the work is done
pails are filled and brimming
over the top with blue, blue, blue.

no clouds in sight, we will squat on the ground
knees bent   ready to take flight
as we watch our mothers — aunties prepare an offering.

every now and again, one will call our name,
sending us off to the forest or the lake
for wood or water, while the rest of us wait our turn.

the next to final step, the laying of fresh boughs
is spice for the gods   earthlings alike.
tâpwî! you will have to believe me.

then blackened potatoes
will be rolled out of the ashes
onto the aromatic willow boughs,

nēpin — Summer

the pot of steaming vegetables
set to the side — just so.
everything has its place here, too.

fresh baked golden bannock
will be placed here and there
and crossed-legged we will wait,

wait for that final touch,
when the pike is laid as centrepiece —
    to heaven we will surely go.

nēpin — Summer

measured time

when horses ran wild, we were   grass tall.
the only sound you could hear then was the thrill
of the early morning songbirds choir
or territorial caw of ravens.

there were few fences
except those to protect your garden
from wayward children and tramping feet of horses,
just paths taking you here   to there.

when horses ran wild, we could   run and hide
all day in the smooth brome, the stampede of hooves
a warning   there were dogs on the loose,
and someone was trying to noose horsepower.

the ponds were full of   frogs and tadpoles,
string-on-a-stick wooden speed boats, launched
for the next long haul from one place
in our imagination   to the next.

the sun shone all day, kissed our faces worthy
as we docked our boats, hauled supplies
to waiting horse-drawn wagons, and then
to their destination   somewhere up the road.

there, we would build our homes from scraps
of lumber and tin close to the edge of the lake-like
pond of tad-fish. we laboured, constructing roads
until empty bellies and mosquito bitten bodies said

no more. the work done, we collected our blocks
of wood, tin and pieces of string
and hid them from duck hunting passers-by
for another day of play   when horses ran wild.

catch me if you can
(another one for nigosis)

he chases after them, round and rolling like
it was   everything. there could never be
too many he says, filling the house,
the yard, and then his room. unsuspecting

I swear there was someone else in the house
with me one night, when one came rolling out
from under the bed. I trip over them
and all I can say is   *lucky for you*

I didn't break my neck. one crawled under
the pillow another night. I couldn't sleep.
and there it was! I found another in the drawer
when I was digging deep, deep down for change.

how many can there possibly be? rubber balls.
bouncy balls. basketballs. baseballs. soft balls.
soccer balls. marbles. round and round,
rolling — *it's madness!* is all I can say.

you think I would have learned my lesson
long ago. the latest toy unwrapped was just that!
your sight set on a ball that rings
as it rolls along on its merry, merry way.

the place where your toes touch mine is a field
for the rolling ball you love so much.
a little bell warning, *it's coming your way!*
it's coming your way! catch me if you can!

nēpin — Summer

something I know

this spring, a male and a female robin
have made the top of the speakers,
wired to feed music to the backyard,
their home.

the giveaway
an audible chirp, chirp
coming from the speakers
every time I walk out the back door.

soon the chicks are visible,
their heads bobbing up
and their mouths wide open
with every click of the door,

mistaking my movements
for that of their parents,
working day and night
to keep their young featherless bellies full.

soon I begin to worry
when the robins do not arrive
to feed their young ones soon enough.
I am concerned about the neighbourhood —

cats lurking.
I am afraid the little ones might fall,
perhaps break their little legs.
my son, who knows me all too well

convinces me to create
a soft landing pad, just in case.
this is the same son who convinced me —
to curb my fear of spiders —

nēpin — Summer

that they wore rubber suction boots
to stay suspended on the ceiling.
so I need not worry so much.
later, I found myself wondering

what will become of me
when the little ones learn to fly?

nēpin — Summer

it grows on trees

the old Manitoba maple is a flutter of birds
chirping, growing wings.
a friend.

it doesn't talk much, just nods
waiting for the next word to fall
out of your mind and onto the page.

it spreads its arms wide, reaching out
in shimmers of green and silver,
and long lost memories of days gone by;

the day Matthew learned to climb,
disappeared into the thicket of its arms
to find a perfect spot to watch the world go by.

it holds a white swing on a limb
built by a woman for her young son,
so he doesn't forget to dream.

every now and again moonlight will catch
a passer-by — a dreamer, a midnight swinger — a child;
laughter clinging in the quiet of night's air

why does the fiddle sound?
(for John Arcand)

why does the fiddle sound so melodious?
poplar trees seem to sway in line,
and clouds obedient float joyous across the sky,
while the sounds of stomping feet   reel
jig, jigging   high above ground.

why does the fiddle sound so distant?
she is all alone behind the shed watching boats go by
motors putt, putting   across the lake,
water rip, rippling   against the shoreline.
a distant memory dancing, her skirt-a-flutter in the wind.

not to be outdone, the sounds of the fast picking
guitar now joins in   ups the tempo; today is
the last day on this earth.   off the grid they go.
oh no, there they go a waltz, waltzing Sarrazin
on rolling logs down, down the river,

duelling life   a certain fall to come.
why does the fiddle sound so sweet?
even those fast asleep floating in the midday sun
are toe-heel tapping   over fiddle strings.
up the tempo just one more time, John!

bring us home!

my grandmother's hands
(*for Brenda McDougall*, one of the family)

grace the cover of a book,
not an ordinary book,
but the book of *miẏo wahkohtowin*
holding sacred our relationships
her arms entwined with sisters.

she was a beautiful woman,
not according to Vanity Fair,
but to a handsome man
who loved her, stayed by her side
for sixty-some short years.

he told me once she was the fairest,
her skin translucent, eyes sky blue
and she was small-boned and graceful like
her father, Robbie — Robbie Gardiner,
an employee of the Hudson's Bay Company.

on the shores and banks of Île à la Crosse
they made a home on Rosser Bay
and then Île Bouleau — their most beloved.
there, they raised their children and grandchildren
they had adopted as their very own.

I remember her   with the purest of silk
between her fingers in one hand,
the softest of white deer hide in the other.
blood, forest, earth, sun and grass yellow
mapping the beauty of her seasons.

I remember her   rolling yards of fabric —
scraps from the garments she made —
recycling and reusing, ahead of her time.
she wove circles, round and round for rugs she made
to keep the winter cold away from our feet.

nēpin — Summer

I remember her fingers joined in prayer,
kneeling — humbled before *le statue du Marrî*
making the sign of the cross with one hand,
a shining rosary clutched tight in the other;
an invocation   trying to restore goodness for all.

I remember her   stirring over a cauldron,
in the quiet of a birch grove
among the rustling aspens and pines;
a wooden ladle in one hand, dried wood
in the other   creating a slow steady burn.

the Great Silence

tonight, a quarter of silver moon clings
and then floats free
from the ragged spruce and jack pines
to the open sky, and there it shines
        blue.   dark.

tonight, the only song you will hear is
earth song —
the distant drum of rapid waters
beckoning — promising a wild, wild ride
down the crashing river and beyond.

blessed, you will be witness
to the haunting serenade of the loon's
bonsoir, bonsoir, mon ami
taking you into the good night.

blessed, you will be witness
to the swish and sway of colourful skirts,
the spirits dancing across the northern sky
a whispering, *kawāpimitin.*

this longing

nothing seems to fill this longing:
neither the generous love of one man, nor
the hoped-for birth of a child.
oh, their love came close, but still I find it larger
in this state of war — this *post nine-eleven.*

I came close when my sisters and I
peed our pants full of joy one summer after
noon, trying our best to catch slithery
morue under rocks along the rugged shoreline
as pets for a day.   *tâpwî!* pets!

I came close playing hide and seek
all day with my cousins — uninterrupted.
we were bushy tailed squirrels climbing trees
and crawling under overturned skiffs
left behind to weather by 'explorers'.

I came close the night we stopped on a busy street,
parked and danced to our favourite song
in full view of strangers driving by —
my heart filled   brimming
but always that moment fleeting.

I came close when I returned to the land
of birch, poplar and supple red willow,
with deer in full flight across the road
and I heard a yester voice echoing, *nitânis,*
I can taste the meat, pan-fried over an open fire.

November sky
(upon reading Louis Riel & Gabriel Dumont *by Joseph Boyden)*

driving home at dusk, billowing white clouds
are painting themselves against a grey sky.
I never pass this way without checking in
on the frozen rider on the river bank
of the South Saskatchewan — flowing swiftly by.

on most days he rides motionless;
perhaps, it's just a state of mind.
tonight, he is draped in a flag of blue white infinity,
a Métis sash gracing his waist, flapping in the wind.

oh, how my heart quickens now to see
his horse galloping long and graceful strides
in time with the billows of a living sky;
the rider in rhythmic stride with his horse.

tonight, even the flag and the sash adorning him
cannot be contained in this November sky.
outnumbered   he rides relentlessly
never afraid of a fight   he prays to the Virgin Mary

his friend Louis will be saved from the gallows.

on nights like this

when darkness falls   the trees
grow long shadows
looming over tar papered shacks
many now call home.

      on nights like this
she can feel their presence,
their white teeth glistening,
bared and ready.

      on nights like this
thcy are loners — spelling danger —
their saber-like teeth
growing out of proportion.

      on nights like this
all she can do is stay awake,
while her siblings rest —
fast asleep.

      on nights like this
all she can do is hold on tight,
in case *ōsimisa* wander out
into the night.

all she can do
is stay close to an open crack
of window   to ready her voice,
hope it doesn't fail her —

remembering Charlie

Charlie is gone. he died.
lonesome.   his aunt said:
he died because of school.

he was malnourished —
his body physically beaten
and psychologically abused —
forbidden to speak Cree.
there is nothing much else to say.
"sorry" doesn't take the pain away.

no one told his mother why.
she wanted to know why
school couldn't be offered
close to his home and family.

he always wanted to be home.
he had a burgundy sweater
he loved.
he had two dogs.
he was twelve.

national anthem
(upon reading A Fair Country *by John Raulston Saul)*

oh, oh Canada
our home and native land . . .

the last time I heard owl's song
I was ten. it was late one evening
along the path — the long way home
over the hill   through red willows.

ôhô was on the limb of a tree
mocking me over and over again.
ooh who, ooh who are you?
no time to respond to a silly old owl.

ooh who, ooh who, indeed! I sing
stealing owl's song tonight
buoyed by the premise *we are all Métis.*
but not so fast John Raulston Saul!

ooh who, ooh who are you, I sing.
say something, something exotic
oh dark, wild mysterious woman.
answer! answer quickly before you forget.

we are the bastard children left behind
by white men and *mixed blood women,*
uncommonly pretty and provocative.
so the his- story books say.

that was not what you wanted to hear!
oh you post-structural, post-colonial sensitive one.
then, I am the obedient subservient.
come ooon!   be a nice, *good brown girl!*

the truth? I am a mass of matter
that matters;
matters to her family.
marrî lapatte — pliable like dough-girl,

falls all over the kitchen counter
can't quite bring it all together;
Julie — a little on the raggedy edge,
sometimes-forgets-to-finish-her-tasks girl.

I am *oui-la* loved,
a name to remember my French heritage;
wāstīyāp is my name from the old ones —
wolf-like eyes shining and all-seeing.

there you have it all now in my
ooh who, ooh who are you song.
I am neither European or Indian — nor
Christopher Columbus' lost song for that matter.

I am *aýisiýino* — a human being;
ewāhkōtoyak — we are all related.
this place knows me — remembers me,
the soft sounds of my grandmothers' tongues.

sing her song, oh, oh Canada!
our home and native land!

wordsong for Ernesto

We climb on the bus, happy to be finally making the trip to the ruins of Chichen Itza, a sacred site of Mayan civilization. Once the young man has successfully corralled all of his charges from their various seaside all-inclusive resorts on the bus, he picks up the microphone and blows on it like one blows on a candle. Wooo!   It crackles.

Good morning! My name is Ernesto. We are so happy you joined us today! We hope to make your trip memorable! Yes, memorable, he repeats. *Chichen Itza is our destination, today. It's a Mayan word,* he explains, *which means 'at the mouth of the well of the enchanted waters'.* He pauses.   *It's a language you may not hear spoken during your visit to this beautiful land. But it is still used today by speakers in this region.*

The Mayan people are alive and well, he says. It sounds like a worn out apology. I listen painfully   *many make their living as they have always done from the land*   *from the sea where they can   whenever they can.*

He doesn't say   disconnected from the bounty of the ocean, now off bounds for the people. He doesn't say displaced from traditional territories, now on roadside allowances. He doesn't say   I am a descendant of the Mayan people. But I know. I have heard that voice   apologetic, afraid to offend.

And then to the joy of his charges, he teaches us the Mayan alphabet. We count. We learn a song — an ancient song. *He!hi! hi! hi!*

The song sung, we fall into a dream state, ancient drums — heart beating time. The warmth of the sun caresses our faces while tall trees conspire   casting long dark snaking shadows on our bodies as we descend into the mouth of the well   under the spell of Itza.

sure as the mighty rivers that flow
(for my friend Dr. Prasad)

he was just an old man who couldn't let go
    once, he was the life-blood.
then, he was considered a visionary
among his peers, among political officials.

but, sure as the mighty rivers that flow — the Ganges,
the Brahmaputra to the Indian Ocean — he was certain
of his own fate. an old man now, he didn't want
to leave this place unsung and unwept.   tonight,

in a moment of reverence, hands held outward
to the living sky, the moon guiding me
to a sacred place,   I remember him. I sing him.
I weep for him. I sing him safely

on the final journey into the beginning of our being.

all about roses and Mary
(for believers)

she came to me, unadorned
on the cover of a book, *Mary of Canada.*
her visits to northwest Saskatchewan unrecorded.
I took her visitation as a sign —

a promise of something better.
what I cannot say. I am sceptical.
my grandmother would be so proud
I had returned to the fold.

that little shrine to Mary that my cousins and I
would carry from house to house (as our duty)
came back to life. we were so happy then
just to be asked   to be together.

the first apparition was September 8, 2002
the day of her birth. according to the records
she appeared in a tiny greenhouse
at the edge of the forest in le Bethlehem du Nord;

site of earliest Catholic missionary activity.
the grey nuns of Montreal in their habits
the Oblates of Mary Immaculate in their dark robes,
a familiar sight on the peninsula long ago.

I remember the grandeur of the bishop's visit,
his royal robes, his gold amethyst ring I never kissed.
many others did, and I wonder now
if I might have missed out on something.

pipon — Winter

I recall followers arriving from surrounding villages
to the shores of Ile à la Crosse. they came
dressed in their finest, in brightly coloured
boats of red, turquoise, purple and canoe-blue.

we were little girl angels then, dressed in white —
making a path of wild rose petals
for the bishop, his priests, the sisters and followers
to the grotto among pine trees built in devotion to Mary of Lourdes.

once there, we perched on our bare knees
on hot rocks in the hot sun of a endless blue sky,
mosquitoes eating us alive, while old Indigenous
Dene and Cree women sang their weeping songs.

in the year 2002, the news of her apparition
in the humble greenhouse spread like fireweed,
hundreds of followers pouring in from beyond
the borders of Saskatchewan, even Canada.

one evening as people gathered for prayer
it is told that *kichitwâ Marrî* appeared again
in a flash of light, as a sign of the cross lit the sky
above the heads of believers.

all they could do was fall on their knees
as a strong scent of roses filled the air.
her beauty striking and radiant, a ghost glow
delivering all to a place of peace.

after the first apparition, others followed
like a plough wind across the whole of northern Saskatchewan.
bible-driven
Joshua of the *Brabant Lake Times*
believed it was a sign from distraction of worldly cares.

pipon — Winter

people have been called to prayer once again, he wrote
as in Fatima on the verge of the Russian revolution,
as in Hrushiv, Ukraine before the disintegration of the USSR,
as in Lourdes amidst the spiritual destruction of the French
Revolution.

I read the priests of the Catholic Church were cautious,
careful in verifying the images miraculous.
the enemy can be cunning, they say.
but the inexplicable is important to them nonetheless

if Sunday mass is packed;
if people are converting and changing their lives.

the explanation of the bible and the church is
not enough to hold me. holy Mary, pray for me!
the bishops would cringe if they knew my mind
that the all powerful goddess stood before me

every day. I see her in her full glory and fury.
she feeds me, clothes me, carries me when I am lost.
she is always forgiving, kind and generous.
she is creation.   she is my mother.

she appeared in a textbook to teach me.
turning the pages of *Mary of Canada,*
I learned she had been everywhere imaginable
on planet earth. I added omissions to the margins (as I always do).

she was there when my ancestors paddled their way
through rivers and lakes, and portages over the land.
they stopped now and then, hats off, heads bowed,
to worship her. They adored her above all

as many others from faraway lands had done,
each time they were delivered from her storms —
her creative urges constantly surging and flowing
life giving, life bearing   life taking.

∞

the sun, the moon and the sky are her kin
the company she keeps while we dream —
our heads turned to the garden of songs
where roses and bluebells are always in full bloom

and white butterflies are shimmering stars in flight
alighting from bloom to bloom.
she's waiting there for you and me
in the sacred mist of time — space eternal

in that ever so delicate balance,   amen.

pipon — Winter

piyak pipon

pipon arrives as expected
with a blanket of snow to cover all her children,
her friend, *oŷôtin kiwîtinohk ohci,* not far behind.

and just moments ago the radio guy —
the righteous one, in a rare moment of awe,
is regaling his listeners with a second-hand tale.

last night, at the height of the fiercest blizzard
to hit Saskatchewan,
temperature hitting record lows,

a family of four was returning home
to their farm from a day of shopping in the city,
when they become stranded on the highway,

after hitting a bank of snow in their path.
it was dark and visibility was poor, when
out of the darkness a figure appeared —

pulling them to safety. and just as it had
appeared, it disappeared
into the storm without a name —

an extended hand   is all they remember.
I remember one winter day, *kaŷâs,*
after a severe winter storm had passed,

snow was piled so high
we had to dig ourselves out.
with small hands I did my part —

believed I could make a difference.
hands can work miracles!

pipon — Winter

surrender
(for Sue Goyette)

when *oẏôtin* is howling outside your window
invite him in, make tea, so grandfather stays for awhile.

when sleep won't come to you on the mountain top,
go to her, promise a poem each day for the rest of your life.

when a wish and a white horse are not in the cards,
play the hand you hold; you are luckier than you think.

when the train whistles you its passing song in the long night,
stop and listen as homage, thankful you can hear its sounding.

when the stereotypical questions you dread arrive,
take flight on a wing and soar above the whole mess.

above all, fiercely love the poem and it will love you back,
let it linger, let it hold you through the long silence.

pipon — Winter

home for Christmas

Home is the place I am whole from the moment I lift my
body off the car seat and land both feet on the ground.
This time covered with snow that squeaks as I walk toward
the front steps. There is a moment of struggle trying to
find the right key in my pocket that I know is there.

As I enter I can almost see my grandfather sitting in his
favourite chair in the far corner. A consummate observer
of the living and the dying, he didn't want to miss a thing.
My grandmother, on the chesterfield, is waiting for her
afternoon tea, her friends, visitors and time. My aunt is
sitting at the kitchen table — my aunt, who is always ready
to create space for another homeless soul. She combs her
hair with a free hand as I walk through the door. I wonder,
now, why she always does this? Is it me — my citified,
stratified, coiffed shoulder length hair that causes this?
Or maybe, it is just to say welcome home *nitânis!* We have
missed you! I have left silk flowers here and there and
figurines in memory of her.

The tightly lipped windows, the tightly clenched doors
have left a musty smell. I hold my breath as I begin a ritual
of vacuuming and dusting, even before I have entered all
the rooms. Then, I stock the shelves with food, make the
beds, and put my clothes into the closet and drawers. I
light a candle, pour myself a glass of wine, and sit there
surveying the richness of my inheritance — a simplicity
of only the necessary: beds to rest the body; closets and
chests of drawers to hide clothing, towels and bedding;
cupboards full of dishes, pots and pans; a hide-a-bed for
company, a table and chairs to greet visitors; old photo-
graphs to remember loved ones; a wooden frame to stretch
mink furs; and, a cross on the wall and the bust of Mary
by the bedside table for salvation.

The candles out, I fall asleep to the world and awaken
the next day to the light of blue and snow. The furnace
cuts itself off and on again. Later, the sun will stream
in through the picture window — the picture window
framing the spruce trees towering over the house, which I
threaten to cut down each time, I am home. Trees planted
by missionaries who arrived here one hundred and fifty
years ago. The trees attract the noisy magpies that flit
gracefully from limb to limb, even on this winter day.

I make a fruit salad for breakfast and sit in my favourite
perch in the kitchen; it seems that I too have a favourite
spot. Later that morning, I pace the floor checking once,
twice, what I have left behind — over-sized sweaters to
keep the cold away, my aunt's sewing kit — just in case,
and books to keep me going. Did I expect someone might
have moved them? Maybe. Maybe, I am hoping deep down
inside that someone, something is alive in this house.
The sun in a low arc in the winter sky plays magic on the
hoarfrost as its melts and frees itself from the large spruce
trees sparkling in the sun as the frost makes its way to
ground. I simply must not cut the trees, even though they
threaten to bring this house down.

In the late afternoon, I find a comfortable spot on the
hide-a-bed and fall into a deep sleep. *Hush, hush, she's
asleep now. Let her sleep,* I hear my grandfather say.

Nap's lament
(dedicated to the memory of Nap Johnston)

I have something important to say

he repeats to the young people
who have come to interview him for posterity.

voice frail and his memory fading,
will anyone care what he thinks?

his mother was a treaty Indian;
his father a white man.

he took the name of the people
who raised him as their very own.

like any young boy his age he cried
when he was left behind in the mission.

his voice welling, he recalls the fire of 1927.
the hill in flames; the boys caught upstairs.

the girls just lucky to be downstairs.
how the people had gathered the bones afterwards.

*they burned to ash flour and they buried them
in one box; there were 27 boys in all,* he says

I have something important to say, he repeats
why do so many young people, today, lie and steal?

*long ago, you could leave your belongings out
without fear they would be taken.*

*where did they learn to be like this?
it cannot be from the people who love them.*

I cry every time I think about it, he says.
what kind of life is it they are choosing to lead?

I can still hear my mother's voice, he says
nigosis, don't wait to be asked . . .

sun dogs on guard

her thoughts are a gale, tossing,
leaping somersaults — a fancy dance
mid-air. someone might be watching,
catching every move she makes

in this mid-morning, winter
snow-sea drifting kind-of-day.
frigid sun dogs guarding as she navigates
a moving line south on highway 11.

spring comes upon her, wanting
the fragrance of roses — John Cabot.
a strange name. like a marker. maybe
to remember something — someone.

a time to awaken. coffee cup in hand,
breezy white pyjamas making the rounds,
unfolding tenderly each and every bud,
talking to the blue irises, robins and jays.

just then the car phone rings,
a return call of crisis — not unexpected.
the voice says, she is home today.
she called in sick. she couldn't take it

anymore, the innuendos — *you are not
good enough* — the backstabbing
backbiting bitch — the gossip
she heard from someone else.

the pain just so   so unbearable.
she didn't know where else to turn.
she said, she awoke one morning
to find the whole wide world

had turned, turned against her.
        to make matters worse,
her husband of twenty-five years
was leaving   seeing another woman

didn't know how to stop himself.
maybe   maybe she needs spring
or someone to bring her a rose — John.
someone to sit with her through the storm.

pipon — Winter

my grub box is empty

a steel guitar from *the deep dark woods*
holds me tonight, a haunting line singing in my ear.
I have something important to say, the voice cries.

but the night slips away — another dry spell.
the pull of the moon can only offer low tide —
pools of water swirling outside my window.

the soft steady flicker of candlelight
is the only company I will have again tonight.
my grub box empty as can be.

pipon — Winter

returning to the silence

I return home tongue tied
by the English language
that seems to slip every now and then,
when I say *ch*urch or *j*am.
God and marmalade
would have been easier
I think to myself, swallowing hard.

but getting sounds right is only half the battle.
a return to the land
of fir trees and muskeg —
its long silences — will require
a different way of being.
I don't need to state the obvious —
the unnecessary, anymore.

my presence   and the meal I cook
for my cousins will be enough.
later, the long silence in our walk
to the graveyard to visit
the loss we carry in our bodies
will be more than we can hold.

the map of my heart

lies somewhere between here
and there. it is not on a piece of paper
carved by the surveyors' pen
for distant monarchies   purveyors

of places and names that do not know me,
but claim to do so — Churchill, Hudson, Mackenzie.
a claim is not a truth etched in stone
forever   a claim is just a piece of paper,

without body   without spirit.
the map of my heart — its contours
shaped by an ice age, lies in the languages
that know me, sing to me, speak to me.   listen.

kiwētinohk — a place signalling the destination
of the ice's retreat. *misinipīyak* – the big bodies of water
I carry on my back are the memories of the people,
the soft rhythms of their knowing.

ikimowuk — it's raining.
imātot — she's crying.
imiẏokisikāk — it's good day.
imiyowātak — she's having a joyful day!
her beauty is a rendering for the lost soul —

the spirit/energy of *pîsim, askî, nipî,*
tipiskâwi pîsim ēkwa acâhkôsuk — stars
are loving angels in the sky
guiding us to *miẏo kisîwâtisowin*

pipon — Winter

blue hue

the morning bathes in a blue hue of snow
breaking dawn.

from bright city lights to the boreal forest
tell-a-vision is a picture window,

days gone by. the mush! mush! mush!
snap of the whip into the wilderness we go

edging our way to the ice ridge
across the frozen lake to the woods.

wolves are creeping toward the fishing hole
to feed on fish scraps left behind;

fisherman, in relationship, had remembered
to leave their offerings behind.

no adults in sight — our worst fear always is
wihtikō . . .

the cracking whip of ice landing us
on the doorstep faster than we can say.

home-safe is *moshōm* waiting
on the shoreline to welcome us back,

from the edge of our imaginings
to the first light of day.

simply, a good day to tell our stories
of the good hunt and life around us.

pipon — Winter

not just another keynote on Indigenous education

one autumn night
antlers flashing in moonlight
I speak to the moose.

flying high above the mountain top,
drawing in its healing power,
I soar with the eagle.

thankful for the day,
for trees that shade and replenish the air,
I sing with raven.

on a sweet scented footpath,
of lowbush cranberries along the river,
I drink her beauty.

gazing out to the ocean,
as her body turned to greet the sun,
I raise my hands   palms upward.

pipon — Winter

reconciliation — a found poem

these days of homecoming
are calling to mind the life of this human family
the faith of this parish.

well over three hundred men and women
religious and clergy came as missionaries
lived among you; some buried here in the local cemetery.

the past few years have been painful
for priests and religious alike, individuals and families
coming to terms with injustice — abuse, accusation and allegation.

there is a burning desire to be set free from what enslaves us.
there is an urgent need for healing and forgiveness.
there is a need for humble confessions and admissions —

facts of history, to extend hands, to let justice flow like a mighty river.
the church has been called upon to examine its mission
having been closely identified with European forces

of expansion and assimilation — the weakening of spirit.
we bear in mind, there has been abuse on both sides
[tâpwî ci — is this the truth; we were children then]

it is for us to look deep in our hearts, to read the signs,
to forge new ways of living together
as men and women of truth.

repentance — an act of honesty and courage.

truth

(upon reading about Métis experiences in residential schools)

we were taken from our mother;
they called her *le savage,*
cut our hair, made us sit on the priest's knee.

silenced by shame, we endured and paid the price,
slowly dying from lack of love —
　　　　from broken hearts.

our men healed us, when they took off their hats
when they listened — heard our stories —
　　　　embraced us.

but still, how can we begin to describe
the indignity — the injury of separation —
of being pulled from a mother's arms?

how can we begin to describe
no words of welcome upon arrival at the mission
to greet six-year old hearts?

how do we begin to describe
no gentle embrace from a mother
to ease the hurts and pains of the day?

where do we find the words?

Notes on the *nakamowin' sa* for the seasons

p. 12   *songs to sing:* Many a paddler has been to the docks in Île à la Crosse; but the docks are no more — only jetties of stones mark the spots. The days of the French voyageurs and free traders are gone except their names and their offspring — Roy, Laliberte, Daigneault, Lariviere, Belanger, Morin, Favel, Malboeuf, Desjarlais, Johnson, Gardiner, Bouvier, etc. The Frobisher's (Thomas and Joseph), Alexander MacKenzie, John Franklin, Peter Pond and David Thompson are but a footnote in this story. From the perspective of this place nothing changes, only the seasons. But everything . . . everything has changed.

p. 29   *one morning after the rain:* This poem is inspired by the description of petroglyphs on the side of a sandstone cliff on the outskirts of St. Victor, in south-central Saskatchewan. The petroglyphs include representations of several symbols — human and animal. No one knows who carved the petroglyphs or why (at least, no one is talking). A petroglyph of a stylized human face catches my interest. After a rain (a time when the petroglyphs appear to show up more clearly), the face appears to be crying. I wonder why?

p. 33   *we must make something of this earth:* "we must make something of this earth" is a line borrowed from Pablo Neruda's poem, "Don't Tell Me" in his collection titled *Epic Song* (1998, English Translation. USA: Azul Editions.)

p. 48   *November sky:* The found words in this poem are from Joseph Boyden's *Louis Riel and Gabriel Dumont* (2010. Toronto: Penguin Canada). The book is part of a series edited by John Ralston Saul on Canadians who have shaped thinking in Canada. The series provides a "personal take" on the lives of these Canadians from the perspective of celebrated contemporary writers.

p. 50   *remembering Charlie:* The found words in this poem are based on a documentary prepared by CBC Jody Porter titled *Dying for an Education.* I was attending high school far away from home and family when the story of twelve-year-old Charlie Wenjack of the Marten Falls First Nation hit the news. He had run away from the Cecelia Jeffrey Indian Residential School in Kenora, Ontario where he was attending school. His body was discovered a week later beside the railway tracks near Redditt, Ontario on October 23, 1966. He was attempting to walk 600 miles back to his home. His parents were not notified when he went missing and they didn't know he was dead until a plane arrived near their home, carrying his body. While his death received national media attention, little changed to address the situation of why so many children were running away from residential schools. I have carried the images and memory of his death for a long time.

p. 53   *wordsong for Ernesto:* This prose poem was written following a trip to the ancient city of Chichen Itza in the Yucatan Peninsula. My son and I had carefully researched the site to learn as much as we could about the sacred well or cenote and the structures we would find there. He was looking forward to visiting the largest "basketball" court (measuring 168 meters long and 70 meters wide) where players tried to hit a 5.4 kilogram rubber ball through stone scoring hoops set high on the court walls. Of particular interest to me was the information that twice a year, during the spring and autumn equinoxes, the setting sun casts a shadow of a serpent writhing down the steps of the Kukulcán pyramid. I was hoping to witness the phenomenon.

p. 55   *all about roses and Mary:* I was inspired to write this poem after reading Joan Skogan's *Mary of Canada* (2003. Canada: Banff Centre Press). I want to acknowledge the "help" of my cousin vye Bouvier on this piece. We had great fun writing back and forth trying to get the factual information 'right' about the apparition of the Virgin Mary in our home community in 2002. We had fun remembering the relationship of the Virgin Mary to ourselves, to our family and to our community. I admit the laughter may have coloured my memory of events somewhat.

p. 63   *Nap's lament:* This was one of the poems created for *Otipimsuak Atlas: Métis People and Lands of Northwest Saskatchewan* (Keith Carlson, Editor, University of Saskatchewan, work in progress). It is based on an interview with the late Nap Johnston of Île à la Crosse.

p. 71   *reconciliation:* With support of First Nations and Inuit organizations, former residential school students took the federal government and churches to court seeking compensation for harm suffered at Indian Residential Schools. Based on consensus reached by the legal counsel of former students, legal council for churches, the Assembly of First Nations, other Aboriginal organizations and the Government of Canada, the case led to the Indian Residential Schools Agreement (2006), the largest class action settlement in Canadian history. It included five different elements: a Common Experience Payment for all eligible former students of Indian Residential Schools, an Independent Assessment Process for claims of sexual or serious physical abuse, measures to support healing, commemorative activities and the establishment of the Truth and Reconciliation Commission. In 2008, the prime minister issued an apology and in 2009, the Vatican expressed its sorrow for the abuses that had occurred. Other churches also expressed their sorrow. In 2009, I returned home to my community of Île-à-la-Crosse to attend Homecoming 1999. At this event, the Oblates of Mary Immaculate issued a statement of apology to all who were present. At the event an artificial rose was offered to each of us. I accepted the rose. "reconciliation" is a found poem, with the exception of one line, which is mine alone.

Glossary of Translations

Note: Where I have decided to use Cree-specific spelling (versus Cree-Michif spelling), I have applied the following source: *nēhiýawēwin: itwēwina*, compiled by Arok Wolvengrey, 2001, Canadian Plains Research Centre, University of Regina, Regina, SK. Volume 2: English — Cree.

a la Grosielle...	the gooseberry–reference to a small island on Île-à-la-Crosse Lake
askiya's..	earth's (Cree- Michif/English blend)
astam..	come here
Bethlehem du Nord..............................	a reference to Île-à-la-Crosse
ēkwa...	and
dadirri...	Australian concept for 'a deep listening' and contemplation that is in tune with the rhythms of the seasons etc.
Île Bouleau..	Birch Island
haka...	a traditional ancestral war cry/dance/challenge of Māori
î pôwâta..	she/he is dreaming
kawāpimitin..	I will see you [again]
kayâs..	long ago
kikcitwâ Marrî....................................	the most revered Mary
kihcikamī...	the big body of water [she carries on her back]
kisîmanitô...	the Great Spirit
kitahtawî kawâpimtonaw...................	perhaps, one day, we will see each other again
kîwîtin...	the north wind
kiýâs, kiýâs, kiýâs...............................	liar, liar, liar
kiýâsak...	gulls
misinipî...	the Churchill River (which means 'the big body of water')
miýo kisîwâtisowin.............................	the goodness of love for one another

miýo wahkohtowin	the goodness of our relationships
morue	cod
moshōm	grandfather
nakamowin'sa	wordsongs (literally, little songs)
nigosis, papīyāhtak	my son, be careful — move in that balanced, respectful way
nisimis	my younger sibling
nitânis	my daughter
ôhô	owl
opâsiwînowak	the people of the narrows
ōsimisa	her younger siblings
oýôtin	the wind
oýôtin kiwîtinohk ohci	the wind from where the ice retreated
pîsim, askî, nipî	sun, earth, water
piyak pipon	one winter
sâkitawahk	Cree place name for Île-à-la-Crosse (which means 'where the rivers meet')
tâpwī	this is true or this is the truth
tipskâwi pîsim,	moon (literally, night sun)
wahkohtowin	being in relationship [with all life]
Waikota	the Maori name of a major river system in the North Island of New Zealand (which means 'the pull of the river current in the sea')
waka taua	war canoes
wihtikō	the hungry one — cannibal

nanāskomowin
Thankfulness and Acknowledgements

It has taken some time to bring a third collection of poetry into being, and as usual, I have many people and organizations to thank for the inspiration and spaces to imagine and to create. Thank you to the Banff Centre (Summer 2011 Self Directed Residency, Spring 2013 Writing With Style and Sue Goyette's Karass). Thank you to the Rene and Allan Dudridge (Summer 2010) and George Jacoby (Spring 2012) for the use of their homes away from home in Victoria and Whistler, respectively. On my last visit to British Columbia, I finally realized why the west coast is a special place for me. It was here that I was re-introduced to my late father, Emile, while he was still in the mink ranching business in Delta, near the Fraser River valley. I recall the many visits I made to the river valley usually at Christmas and Easter — times of never ending mists and rain.

As much as I rely on an intuitive response to life around me to create, relationships and events that affect our lives as human beings have also served to provide a sense of urgency and at times agency to record moments of our humanity and transgressions. Fortunate circumstances have also conspired to take me into hiding, so I can find that dreaming place to write poetry. One such circumstance is the joint project of the University of Saskatchewan and the University of Alberta on the Métis of Northwest Saskatchewan. As always, I armed myself with various books, in case I hit the wall. One book deserves special mention, *Songs of Manitoba*, by Margaret Arnett MacLeod, published by Ryerson Press in 1959. The book is a collection of folk songs, local to the Red River, although the music is not from the area. The famous Pierre Falcon, poet of the Métis, composed many of the songs in the collection. How it came to my possession is also a special story. On one of those visits to the west coast, I called up my friend Brenda Ireland for a visit. She arrived with a gift in hand. The *Songs of Manitoba* was a find in one of those weekend yard sales. She bought it knowing I would appreciate it — I do. The audiotapes of Elders from my home community of Île-à-la-Crosse provided to me by the University of Saskatchewan also provided inspiration. Although the Elders are now in the spirit world, I am humbled to have had the privilege of hearing their voices. I hope I have honoured them with my *nakamowin'sa* — my wordsongs (literally "little songs").

Selections (revised) in this collection were created for *Otipimsuak Atlas: Métis People and Lands of Northwest Saskatchewan* (Keith Carlson, Editor, University of Saskatchewan, work in progress).

Thank you to Gregory Scofield, Nancy Van Styvendale and Sheelah Mclean for "reading" my poetry in advance and offering their kind words. Thank you to my friend and colleague, Vince Ahenakew, for his Cree-Michif guidance with the *Glossary in Translations*. Thank you to my poetic friends: Lloyd Ratzlaff for his encouragement, Viz Ink mates — you know who you are (2011 – present) and to Sue Goyette's Karass (Spring 2013) for their 'undoing', and invitations to rethink each and every word. Thank you to Thistledown Press — to Al Forrie and Jackie Forrie and their staff — for their support and artistry in bringing my words to print. Finally, *maarsi* to Elizabeth Philips the poet and the editor of this collection! I had always admired this mystery woman who is quick of wit, intelligence, and generosity. Without her sage advise tucked in the back of my mind in the spring of 2013, I might have made a grander fool of myself at the Calgary airport. No, I didn't leave my job, my family, or move half way around the world, but I was overcome by the sale of Indigenous goods made in China!